cRowned.

SET IN SOUL

© 2017 Tatiana Media LLC in partnership with Set In Soul LLC

ISBN #: 978-0-9971153-6-9

Published by Tatiana Media LLC

For general information on our other products and services, please contact our Customer Support within the United States at support@setinsoul.com.

Tatiana Media LLC as well as Set In Soul LLC publishes its books in a variety of electronic formats. Some content that appears in print may not be available in electronic books.

THIS JOURNAL BELONGS TO

_____

DEDICATED TO
WHO I AM BECOMING

TABLE OF CONTENTS

HOW TO USE THIS JOURNAL

It's time to get back to you. It's time to really dig down and figure out what you mean to yourself, as well as who are you becoming and if you like who you are turning into. You can go around asking everyone how they are doing, but do you really take the time to ask yourself that same question? Do you show up for yourself mentally, spiritually, emotionally and physically? When was the last time you asked yourself 'are you okay?' 'do you need anything today?' 'what can I provide myself with today?' All these questions and more are a part of self care and self love. If you haven't taken the time to really put yourself first, to invest in yourself or grow from where you are, now is the time to do it. This journal was created with the intent to assist in restoring self confidence, as well as gaining inner strength, and establishing a new way to care for self. It is in this journal that you will be forced to listen to your inner self and what your spirit within needs. It is with the words you write within this journal, that will help you to become your own best friend.

This journal covers one hundred and fifty days of you growing closer to you. It is recommended that you fill out this journal daily. There is a section to fill in both morning and night. You will want to make it a habit to think about your wellbeing first until it becomes something that you organically do. The purpose of this journal is to reintroduce you to yourself. Build a healthier, happier and stronger connection with not only the person you see yourself being, but in accepting who you are right now. In order to heal, let go, move forward, and claim your blessings, you must realize you are worthy, important and valued.

cRowned is the journal that will bring light to how to love yourself and compliment yourself. You will be required to dig down deep to explore what makes you happy, what you need more of and what you need less of in order to fully operate in your best you. The quotes throughout this journal are there to motivate and encourage you along your path. If needed, cut the quotes out and hang them on your wall as a reminder of who you are. The more you see the quotes, read the quotes and repeat them to yourself, the more confidence and love you are giving to your inner you. It is your time to be the best you can be. Use the blank spaces to write some thoughts towards yourself with what you are currently feeling and what you need. Pair this journal with your daily morning self care routine and you are well on your way to a new and improved you.

This is your time as you have already been cRowned. So take your place and reposition your love to you.

INTROSPECTION

What I Love About Me:

What Excites Me:

The Motto I Live By:

What Interest Me:

I Need To Work On:

INTROSPECTION

I Am Currently Happy With:

If I Am Not Happy, What Stands Between Me And My Happiness?

I Am Passionate About:

I Value:

I Really Want:

INTROSPECTION

What I Believe About Myself:

In The Past, I Have Always Thought:

My Strength Lies In:

My Weakness Is:

The Truth About Me Is:

INTROSPECTION

I Am Sensitive About:

I Have Grown To Become Better At:

The Things I Keep Sacred To Me:

What I Would Like To Change About Myself:

Some Of The Best Moments Of My Life Thus Far Are:

INTROSPECTION

I Stopped Doing:

I Started Doing:

I'm At A Place In Life Where:

What Fullfils Me:

When I Am Feeling Bad, I Change The Way I Am Feeling By:

INTROSPECTION

How Could I Spice Up My Life?

I Express My Needs By:

What I Need Right Now:

What Do I Value Most About Me?

What Makes Me Laugh?

INTROSPECTION

What Makes Me Smile?

What Hurts Me?

What Makes Me Cry?

What Makes Me Doubt Myself?

What Does Confidence Mean To Me?

INTROSPECTION

What Caused Me To Lose Confidence?

Do I Compare Myself To Others?

I Tend To My Spiritual Needs By:

I Tend To My Physical Needs By:

I Tend To My Emotional Needs By:

INTROSPECTION

Am I Emotionally Balanced?

What Can I Do To Get Emotionally Balanced?

What Changes Can I Make To Have A Stronger Relationship With Myself:

I Fell In Love With:

What Does Unconditional Self Love Look Like?

INTROSPECTION

What Is My Self Care Regime?

I Typically Wake Up Feeling:

My External Space Looks And Feels Like:

Current Beliefs That I Need To Get Rid Of That Is Preventing Me From Fully Loving Myself:

What Makes Me Irreplaceable?

INTROSPECTION

Some Achievements That I Have Accomplished That Make Me Proud Are:

What Is Currently Stopping Me From Pursing My Goals And Dreams?

Currently I Have Put This Element Of My Life On Hold:

What I Fear Most In My Life:

What I Am Changing About This Fear:

REPOSITIONING MY LOVE

MORNING THOUGHTS

Today: Mood:

Today's Prayer For Myself:

Today I Am Repeating To Myself:

What I Am Doing For Myself Today:

NIGHTLY THOUGHTS

Today's Inner Self Care Regime Included:

I Am Happy I Did:

Today I Gave Myself The Following Compliment:

Today I Was Inspired By:

I Increased My Confidence By:

Today I Protected My Space By:

MORNING THOUGHTS

Today: Mood:

Today's Prayer For Myself:

Today I Am Repeating To Myself:

What I Am Doing For Myself Today:

NIGHTLY THOUGHTS

Today's Inner Self Care Regime Included:

I Am Happy I Did:

Today I Gave Myself The Following Compliment:

Today I Was Inspired By:

I Increased My Confidence By:

Today I Protected My Space By:

MORNING THOUGHTS

Today: Mood:

Today's Prayer For Myself:

Today I Am Repeating To Myself:

What I Am Doing For Myself Today:

NIGHTLY THOUGHTS

Today's Inner Self Care Regime Included:

I Am Happy I Did:

Today I Gave Myself The Following Compliment:

Today I Was Inspired By:

I Increased My Confidence By:

Today I Protected My Space By:

MORNING THOUGHTS

Today: Mood:

Today's Prayer For Myself:

Today I Am Repeating To Myself:

What I Am Doing For Myself Today:

NIGHTLY THOUGHTS

Today's Inner Self Care Regime Included:

I Am Happy I Did:

Today I Gave Myself The Following Compliment:

Today I Was Inspired By:

I Increased My Confidence By:

Today I Protected My Space By:

MORNING THOUGHTS

Today: Mood:

Today's Prayer For Myself:

Today I Am Repeating To Myself:

What I Am Doing For Myself Today:

NIGHTLY THOUGHTS

Today's Inner Self Care Regime Included:

I Am Happy I Did:

Today I Gave Myself The Following Compliment:

Today I Was Inspired By:

I Increased My Confidence By:

Today I Protected My Space By:

Self
LOVE

Is Self Care.

MORNING THOUGHTS

Today: Mood:

Today's Prayer For Myself:

Today I Am Repeating To Myself:

What I Am Doing For Myself Today:

NIGHTLY THOUGHTS

Today's Inner Self Care Regime Included:

I Am Happy I Did:

Today I Gave Myself The Following Compliment:

Today I Was Inspired By:

I Increased My Confidence By:

Today I Protected My Space By:

MORNING THOUGHTS

Today: Mood:

Today's Prayer For Myself:

Today I Am Repeating To Myself:

What I Am Doing For Myself Today:

NIGHTLY THOUGHTS

Today's Inner Self Care Regime Included:

I Am Happy I Did:

Today I Gave Myself The Following Compliment:

Today I Was Inspired By:

I Increased My Confidence By:

Today I Protected My Space By:

DID I TAKE THE TIME TO LISTEN TO MY SPIRIT TODAY? WAS I OBEDIENT TO IT?

MORNING THOUGHTS

Today: Mood:

Today's Prayer For Myself:

Today I Am Repeating To Myself:

What I Am Doing For Myself Today:

NIGHTLY THOUGHTS

Today's Inner Self Care Regime Included:

I Am Happy I Did:

Today I Gave Myself The Following Compliment:

Today I Was Inspired By:

I Increased My Confidence By:

Today I Protected My Space By:

MORNING THOUGHTS

Today: Mood:

Today's Prayer For Myself:

Today I Am Repeating To Myself:

What I Am Doing For Myself Today:

NIGHTLY THOUGHTS

Today's Inner Self Care Regime Included:

I Am Happy I Did:

Today I Gave Myself The Following Compliment:

Today I Was Inspired By:

I Increased My Confidence By:

Today I Protected My Space By:

MORNING THOUGHTS

Today: Mood:

Today's Prayer For Myself:

Today I Am Repeating To Myself:

What I Am Doing For Myself Today:

NIGHTLY THOUGHTS

Today's Inner Self Care Regime Included:

I Am Happy I Did:

Today I Gave Myself The Following Compliment:

Today I Was Inspired By:

I Increased My Confidence By:

Today I Protected My Space By:

Everything You
Are Ready To Do For
SOMEONE
Else, Be Willing To Do For Yourself.

MORNING THOUGHTS

Today: Mood:

Today's Prayer For Myself:

Today I Am Repeating To Myself:

What I Am Doing For Myself Today:

NIGHTLY THOUGHTS

Today's Inner Self Care Regime Included:

I Am Happy I Did:

Today I Gave Myself The Following Compliment:

Today I Was Inspired By:

I Increased My Confidence By:

Today I Protected My Space By:

MORNING THOUGHTS

Today: Mood:

Today's Prayer For Myself:

Today I Am Repeating To Myself:

What I Am Doing For Myself Today:

NIGHTLY THOUGHTS

Today's Inner Self Care Regime Included:

I Am Happy I Did:

Today I Gave Myself The Following Compliment:

Today I Was Inspired By:

I Increased My Confidence By:

Today I Protected My Space By:

MORNING THOUGHTS

Today: Mood:

Today's Prayer For Myself:

Today I Am Repeating To Myself:

What I Am Doing For Myself Today:

NIGHTLY THOUGHTS

Today's Inner Self Care Regime Included:

I Am Happy I Did:

Today I Gave Myself The Following Compliment:

Today I Was Inspired By:

I Increased My Confidence By:

Today I Protected My Space By:

MORNING THOUGHTS

Today: Mood:

Today's Prayer For Myself:

Today I Am Repeating To Myself:

What I Am Doing For Myself Today:

NIGHTLY THOUGHTS

Today's Inner Self Care Regime Included:

I Am Happy I Did:

Today I Gave Myself The Following Compliment:

Today I Was Inspired By:

I Increased My Confidence By:

Today I Protected My Space By:

I LOVE WHEN

MORNING THOUGHTS

Today: Mood:

Today's Prayer For Myself:

Today I Am Repeating To Myself:

What I Am Doing For Myself Today:

NIGHTLY THOUGHTS

Today's Inner Self Care Regime Included:

I Am Happy I Did:

Today I Gave Myself The Following Compliment:

Today I Was Inspired By:

I Increased My Confidence By:

Today I Protected My Space By:

MORNING THOUGHTS

Today: Mood:

Today's Prayer For Myself:

Today I Am Repeating To Myself:

What I Am Doing For Myself Today:

NIGHTLY THOUGHTS

Today's Inner Self Care Regime Included:

I Am Happy I Did:

Today I Gave Myself The Following Compliment:

Today I Was Inspired By:

I Increased My Confidence By:

Today I Protected My Space By:

MORNING THOUGHTS

Today: Mood:

Today's Prayer For Myself:

Today I Am Repeating To Myself:

What I Am Doing For Myself Today:

NIGHTLY THOUGHTS

Today's Inner Self Care Regime Included:

I Am Happy I Did:

Today I Gave Myself The Following Compliment:

Today I Was Inspired By:

I Increased My Confidence By:

Today I Protected My Space By:

MORNING THOUGHTS

Today: Mood:

Today's Prayer For Myself:

Today I Am Repeating To Myself:

What I Am Doing For Myself Today:

NIGHTLY THOUGHTS

Today's Inner Self Care Regime Included:

I Am Happy I Did:

Today I Gave Myself The Following Compliment:

Today I Was Inspired By:

I Increased My Confidence By:

Today I Protected My Space By:

You Have Survived What
Was Suppose To Harm You,

EMBARRASS
YOU,

Destroy You And Play You.
Look At You. That Crown
Never Comes Off.

MORNING THOUGHTS

Today: Mood:

Today's Prayer For Myself:

Today I Am Repeating To Myself:

What I Am Doing For Myself Today:

NIGHTLY THOUGHTS

Today's Inner Self Care Regime Included:

I Am Happy I Did:

Today I Gave Myself The Following Compliment:

Today I Was Inspired By:

I Increased My Confidence By:

Today I Protected My Space By:

MORNING THOUGHTS

Today: Mood:

Today's Prayer For Myself:

Today I Am Repeating To Myself:

What I Am Doing For Myself Today:

NIGHTLY THOUGHTS

Today's Inner Self Care Regime Included:

I Am Happy I Did:

Today I Gave Myself The Following Compliment:

Today I Was Inspired By:

I Increased My Confidence By:

Today I Protected My Space By:

MORNING THOUGHTS

Today: Mood:

Today's Prayer For Myself:

Today I Am Repeating To Myself:

What I Am Doing For Myself Today:

NIGHTLY THOUGHTS

Today's Inner Self Care Regime Included:

I Am Happy I Did:

Today I Gave Myself The Following Compliment:

Today I Was Inspired By:

I Increased My Confidence By:

Today I Protected My Space By:

MORNING THOUGHTS

Today: Mood:

Today's Prayer For Myself:

Today I Am Repeating To Myself:

What I Am Doing For Myself Today:

NIGHTLY THOUGHTS

Today's Inner Self Care Regime Included:

I Am Happy I Did:

Today I Gave Myself The Following Compliment:

Today I Was Inspired By:

I Increased My Confidence By:

Today I Protected My Space By:

MORNING THOUGHTS

Today: Mood:

Today's Prayer For Myself:

Today I Am Repeating To Myself:

What I Am Doing For Myself Today:

NIGHTLY THOUGHTS

Today's Inner Self Care Regime Included:

I Am Happy I Did:

Today I Gave Myself The Following Compliment:

Today I Was Inspired By:

I Increased My Confidence By:

Today I Protected My Space By:

I've Upgraded My

MIND,

My Spirit And My
Standards. I've Got This.

WHAT AM I DOING FOR ME?

MORNING THOUGHTS

Today: Mood:

Today's Prayer For Myself:

Today I Am Repeating To Myself:

What I Am Doing For Myself Today:

NIGHTLY THOUGHTS

Today's Inner Self Care Regime Included:

I Am Happy I Did:

Today I Gave Myself The Following Compliment:

Today I Was Inspired By:

I Increased My Confidence By:

Today I Protected My Space By:

MORNING THOUGHTS

Today: Mood:

Today's Prayer For Myself:

Today I Am Repeating To Myself:

What I Am Doing For Myself Today:

NIGHTLY THOUGHTS

Today's Inner Self Care Regime Included:

I Am Happy I Did:

Today I Gave Myself The Following Compliment:

Today I Was Inspired By:

I Increased My Confidence By:

Today I Protected My Space By:

MORNING THOUGHTS

Today: Mood:

Today's Prayer For Myself:

Today I Am Repeating To Myself:

What I Am Doing For Myself Today:

NIGHTLY THOUGHTS

Today's Inner Self Care Regime Included:

I Am Happy I Did:

Today I Gave Myself The Following Compliment:

Today I Was Inspired By:

I Increased My Confidence By:

Today I Protected My Space By:

MORNING THOUGHTS

Today: Mood:

Today's Prayer For Myself:

Today I Am Repeating To Myself:

What I Am Doing For Myself Today:

NIGHTLY THOUGHTS

Today's Inner Self Care Regime Included:

I Am Happy I Did:

Today I Gave Myself The Following Compliment:

Today I Was Inspired By:

I Increased My Confidence By:

Today I Protected My Space By:

HOW DID I SHOW LOVE TO MYSELF TODAY?

MORNING THOUGHTS

Today: Mood:

Today's Prayer For Myself:

Today I Am Repeating To Myself:

What I Am Doing For Myself Today:

NIGHTLY THOUGHTS

Today's Inner Self Care Regime Included:

I Am Happy I Did:

Today I Gave Myself The Following Compliment:

Today I Was Inspired By:

I Increased My Confidence By:

Today I Protected My Space By:

MORNING THOUGHTS

Today: Mood:

Today's Prayer For Myself:

Today I Am Repeating To Myself:

What I Am Doing For Myself Today:

NIGHTLY THOUGHTS

Today's Inner Self Care Regime Included:

I Am Happy I Did:

Today I Gave Myself The Following Compliment:

Today I Was Inspired By:

I Increased My Confidence By:

Today I Protected My Space By:

MORNING THOUGHTS

Today: Mood:

Today's Prayer For Myself:

Today I Am Repeating To Myself:

What I Am Doing For Myself Today:

NIGHTLY THOUGHTS

Today's Inner Self Care Regime Included:

I Am Happy I Did:

Today I Gave Myself The Following Compliment:

Today I Was Inspired By:

I Increased My Confidence By:

Today I Protected My Space By:

MY
HEART

Is In The Right Place.
It's Now In My Hands.

MORNING THOUGHTS

Today: Mood:

Today's Prayer For Myself:

Today I Am Repeating To Myself:

What I Am Doing For Myself Today:

NIGHTLY THOUGHTS

Today's Inner Self Care Regime Included:

I Am Happy I Did:

Today I Gave Myself The Following Compliment:

Today I Was Inspired By:

I Increased My Confidence By:

Today I Protected My Space By:

MORNING THOUGHTS

Today: Mood:

Today's Prayer For Myself:

Today I Am Repeating To Myself:

What I Am Doing For Myself Today:

NIGHTLY THOUGHTS

Today's Inner Self Care Regime Included:

I Am Happy I Did:

Today I Gave Myself The Following Compliment:

Today I Was Inspired By:

I Increased My Confidence By:

Today I Protected My Space By:

MORNING THOUGHTS

Today: Mood:

Today's Prayer For Myself:

Today I Am Repeating To Myself:

What I Am Doing For Myself Today:

NIGHTLY THOUGHTS

Today's Inner Self Care Regime Included:

I Am Happy I Did:

Today I Gave Myself The Following Compliment:

Today I Was Inspired By:

I Increased My Confidence By:

Today I Protected My Space By:

MORNING THOUGHTS

Today: Mood:

Today's Prayer For Myself:

Today I Am Repeating To Myself:

What I Am Doing For Myself Today:

NIGHTLY THOUGHTS

Today's Inner Self Care Regime Included:

I Am Happy I Did:

Today I Gave Myself The Following Compliment:

Today I Was Inspired By:

I Increased My Confidence By:

Today I Protected My Space By:

MORNING THOUGHTS

Today: Mood:

Today's Prayer For Myself:

Today I Am Repeating To Myself:

What I Am Doing For Myself Today:

NIGHTLY THOUGHTS

Today's Inner Self Care Regime Included:

I Am Happy I Did:

Today I Gave Myself The Following Compliment:

Today I Was Inspired By:

I Increased My Confidence By:

Today I Protected My Space By:

MORNING THOUGHTS

Today: Mood:

Today's Prayer For Myself:

Today I Am Repeating To Myself:

What I Am Doing For Myself Today:

NIGHTLY THOUGHTS

Today's Inner Self Care Regime Included:

I Am Happy I Did:

Today I Gave Myself The Following Compliment:

Today I Was Inspired By:

I Increased My Confidence By:

Today I Protected My Space By:

Everyday I Find
SOMETHING
NEW
To Love About Me.

I Accept The

OLD
ME

Because It
Brought The
New Me.

MORNING THOUGHTS

Today: Mood:

Today's Prayer For Myself:

Today I Am Repeating To Myself:

What I Am Doing For Myself Today:

NIGHTLY THOUGHTS

Today's Inner Self Care Regime Included:

I Am Happy I Did:

Today I Gave Myself The Following Compliment:

Today I Was Inspired By:

I Increased My Confidence By:

Today I Protected My Space By:

MORNING THOUGHTS

Today: Mood:

Today's Prayer For Myself:

Today I Am Repeating To Myself:

What I Am Doing For Myself Today:

NIGHTLY THOUGHTS

Today's Inner Self Care Regime Included:

I Am Happy I Did:

Today I Gave Myself The Following Compliment:

Today I Was Inspired By:

I Increased My Confidence By:

Today I Protected My Space By:

MORNING THOUGHTS

Today: Mood:

Today's Prayer For Myself:

Today I Am Repeating To Myself:

What I Am Doing For Myself Today:

NIGHTLY THOUGHTS

Today's Inner Self Care Regime Included:

I Am Happy I Did:

Today I Gave Myself The Following Compliment:

Today I Was Inspired By:

I Increased My Confidence By:

Today I Protected My Space By:

HOW DID I SHOW LOVE TO MY BODY TODAY?

MORNING THOUGHTS

Today: Mood:

Today's Prayer For Myself:

Today I Am Repeating To Myself:

What I Am Doing For Myself Today:

NIGHTLY THOUGHTS

Today's Inner Self Care Regime Included:

I Am Happy I Did:

Today I Gave Myself The Following Compliment:

Today I Was Inspired By:

I Increased My Confidence By:

Today I Protected My Space By:

MORNING THOUGHTS

Today: Mood:

Today's Prayer For Myself:

Today I Am Repeating To Myself:

What I Am Doing For Myself Today:

NIGHTLY THOUGHTS

Today's Inner Self Care Regime Included:

I Am Happy I Did:

Today I Gave Myself The Following Compliment:

Today I Was Inspired By:

I Increased My Confidence By:

Today I Protected My Space By:

MUSE.

That Is Who I Am To Me.

MORNING THOUGHTS

Today: Mood:

Today's Prayer For Myself:

Today I Am Repeating To Myself:

What I Am Doing For Myself Today:

NIGHTLY THOUGHTS

Today's Inner Self Care Regime Included:

I Am Happy I Did:

Today I Gave Myself The Following Compliment:

Today I Was Inspired By:

I Increased My Confidence By:

Today I Protected My Space By:

MORNING THOUGHTS

Today: Mood:

Today's Prayer For Myself:

Today I Am Repeating To Myself:

What I Am Doing For Myself Today:

NIGHTLY THOUGHTS

Today's Inner Self Care Regime Included:

I Am Happy I Did:

Today I Gave Myself The Following Compliment:

Today I Was Inspired By:

I Increased My Confidence By:

Today I Protected My Space By:

MORNING THOUGHTS

Today: Mood:

Today's Prayer For Myself:

Today I Am Repeating To Myself:

What I Am Doing For Myself Today:

NIGHTLY THOUGHTS

Today's Inner Self Care Regime Included:

I Am Happy I Did:

Today I Gave Myself The Following Compliment:

Today I Was Inspired By:

I Increased My Confidence By:

Today I Protected My Space By:

MORNING THOUGHTS

Today: Mood:

Today's Prayer For Myself:

Today I Am Repeating To Myself:

What I Am Doing For Myself Today:

NIGHTLY THOUGHTS

Today's Inner Self Care Regime Included:

I Am Happy I Did:

Today I Gave Myself The Following Compliment:

Today I Was Inspired By:

I Increased My Confidence By:

Today I Protected My Space By:

TODAY'S SELF
PRAYER

MORNING THOUGHTS

Today: Mood:

Today's Prayer For Myself:

Today I Am Repeating To Myself:

What I Am Doing For Myself Today:

NIGHTLY THOUGHTS

Today's Inner Self Care Regime Included:

I Am Happy I Did:

Today I Gave Myself The Following Compliment:

Today I Was Inspired By:

I Increased My Confidence By:

Today I Protected My Space By:

MORNING THOUGHTS

Today: Mood:

Today's Prayer For Myself:

Today I Am Repeating To Myself:

What I Am Doing For Myself Today:

NIGHTLY THOUGHTS

Today's Inner Self Care Regime Included:

I Am Happy I Did:

Today I Gave Myself The Following Compliment:

Today I Was Inspired By:

I Increased My Confidence By:

Today I Protected My Space By:

MORNING THOUGHTS

Today: Mood:

Today's Prayer For Myself:

Today I Am Repeating To Myself:

What I Am Doing For Myself Today:

NIGHTLY THOUGHTS

Today's Inner Self Care Regime Included:

I Am Happy I Did:

Today I Gave Myself The Following Compliment:

Today I Was Inspired By:

I Increased My Confidence By:

Today I Protected My Space By:

MORNING THOUGHTS

Today: Mood:

Today's Prayer For Myself:

Today I Am Repeating To Myself:

What I Am Doing For Myself Today:

NIGHTLY THOUGHTS

Today's Inner Self Care Regime Included:

I Am Happy I Did:

Today I Gave Myself The Following Compliment:

Today I Was Inspired By:

I Increased My Confidence By:

Today I Protected My Space By:

The Doors That I Onced

PRAYED

Would Open Are Now Opening.

MORNING THOUGHTS

Today: Mood:

Today's Prayer For Myself:

Today I Am Repeating To Myself:

What I Am Doing For Myself Today:

NIGHTLY THOUGHTS

Today's Inner Self Care Regime Included:

I Am Happy I Did:

Today I Gave Myself The Following Compliment:

Today I Was Inspired By:

I Increased My Confidence By:

Today I Protected My Space By:

MORNING THOUGHTS

Today: Mood:

Today's Prayer For Myself:

Today I Am Repeating To Myself:

What I Am Doing For Myself Today:

NIGHTLY THOUGHTS

Today's Inner Self Care Regime Included:

I Am Happy I Did:

Today I Gave Myself The Following Compliment:

Today I Was Inspired By:

I Increased My Confidence By:

Today I Protected My Space By:

MORNING THOUGHTS

Today: Mood:

Today's Prayer For Myself:

Today I Am Repeating To Myself:

What I Am Doing For Myself Today:

NIGHTLY THOUGHTS

Today's Inner Self Care Regime Included:

I Am Happy I Did:

Today I Gave Myself The Following Compliment:

Today I Was Inspired By:

I Increased My Confidence By:

Today I Protected My Space By:

I AM WORKING TO OVERCOME

MORNING THOUGHTS

Today: Mood:

Today's Prayer For Myself:

Today I Am Repeating To Myself:

What I Am Doing For Myself Today:

NIGHTLY THOUGHTS

Today's Inner Self Care Regime Included:

I Am Happy I Did:

Today I Gave Myself The Following Compliment:

Today I Was Inspired By:

I Increased My Confidence By:

Today I Protected My Space By:

MORNING THOUGHTS

Today: Mood:

Today's Prayer For Myself:

Today I Am Repeating To Myself:

What I Am Doing For Myself Today:

NIGHTLY THOUGHTS

Today's Inner Self Care Regime Included:

I Am Happy I Did:

Today I Gave Myself The Following Compliment:

Today I Was Inspired By:

I Increased My Confidence By:

Today I Protected My Space By:

MORNING THOUGHTS

Today: Mood:

Today's Prayer For Myself:

Today I Am Repeating To Myself:

What I Am Doing For Myself Today:

NIGHTLY THOUGHTS

Today's Inner Self Care Regime Included:

I Am Happy I Did:

Today I Gave Myself The Following Compliment:

Today I Was Inspired By:

I Increased My Confidence By:

Today I Protected My Space By:

I LOVE Myself For No Reason.
I LOVE Myself For Every Reason.

MORNING THOUGHTS

Today: Mood:

Today's Prayer For Myself:

Today I Am Repeating To Myself:

What I Am Doing For Myself Today:

NIGHTLY THOUGHTS

Today's Inner Self Care Regime Included:

I Am Happy I Did:

Today I Gave Myself The Following Compliment:

Today I Was Inspired By:

I Increased My Confidence By:

Today I Protected My Space By:

MORNING THOUGHTS

Today: Mood:

Today's Prayer For Myself:

Today I Am Repeating To Myself:

What I Am Doing For Myself Today:

NIGHTLY THOUGHTS

Today's Inner Self Care Regime Included:

I Am Happy I Did:

Today I Gave Myself The Following Compliment:

Today I Was Inspired By:

I Increased My Confidence By:

Today I Protected My Space By:

MORNING THOUGHTS

Today: Mood:

Today's Prayer For Myself:

Today I Am Repeating To Myself:

What I Am Doing For Myself Today:

NIGHTLY THOUGHTS

Today's Inner Self Care Regime Included:

I Am Happy I Did:

Today I Gave Myself The Following Compliment:

Today I Was Inspired By:

I Increased My Confidence By:

Today I Protected My Space By:

MORNING THOUGHTS

Today: Mood:

Today's Prayer For Myself:

Today I Am Repeating To Myself:

What I Am Doing For Myself Today:

NIGHTLY THOUGHTS

Today's Inner Self Care Regime Included:

I Am Happy I Did:

Today I Gave Myself The Following Compliment:

Today I Was Inspired By:

I Increased My Confidence By:

Today I Protected My Space By:

MY THOUGHTS ON MY PROGRESSION IN LIFE

MORNING THOUGHTS

Today: Mood:

Today's Prayer For Myself:

Today I Am Repeating To Myself:

What I Am Doing For Myself Today:

NIGHTLY THOUGHTS

Today's Inner Self Care Regime Included:

I Am Happy I Did:

Today I Gave Myself The Following Compliment:

Today I Was Inspired By:

I Increased My Confidence By:

Today I Protected My Space By:

MORNING THOUGHTS

Today: Mood:

Today's Prayer For Myself:

Today I Am Repeating To Myself:

What I Am Doing For Myself Today:

NIGHTLY THOUGHTS

Today's Inner Self Care Regime Included:

I Am Happy I Did:

Today I Gave Myself The Following Compliment:

Today I Was Inspired By:

I Increased My Confidence By:

Today I Protected My Space By:

MORNING THOUGHTS

Today: Mood:

Today's Prayer For Myself:

Today I Am Repeating To Myself:

What I Am Doing For Myself Today:

NIGHTLY THOUGHTS

Today's Inner Self Care Regime Included:

I Am Happy I Did:

Today I Gave Myself The Following Compliment:

Today I Was Inspired By:

I Increased My Confidence By:

Today I Protected My Space By:

MORNING THOUGHTS

Today: Mood:

Today's Prayer For Myself:

Today I Am Repeating To Myself:

What I Am Doing For Myself Today:

NIGHTLY THOUGHTS

Today's Inner Self Care Regime Included:

I Am Happy I Did:

Today I Gave Myself The Following Compliment:

Today I Was Inspired By:

I Increased My Confidence By:

Today I Protected My Space By:

MORNING THOUGHTS

Today: Mood:

Today's Prayer For Myself:

Today I Am Repeating To Myself:

What I Am Doing For Myself Today:

NIGHTLY THOUGHTS

Today's Inner Self Care Regime Included:

I Am Happy I Did:

Today I Gave Myself The Following Compliment:

Today I Was Inspired By:

I Increased My Confidence By:

Today I Protected My Space By:

MORNING THOUGHTS

Today: Mood:

Today's Prayer For Myself:

Today I Am Repeating To Myself:

What I Am Doing For Myself Today:

NIGHTLY THOUGHTS

Today's Inner Self Care Regime Included:

I Am Happy I Did:

Today I Gave Myself The Following Compliment:

Today I Was Inspired By:

I Increased My Confidence By:

Today I Protected My Space By:

I Am
Focused
On My Life.

I'M
FOCUSED

On Doing What's Best For Me. I'm
Focused On Being The Best Me.
I'm Focused On Loving Me. I'm
Focused On What Motivates Me.
I'm Focused On The Positive And
That Is The Only Thing That Matters
Right Now.

POSITIVE
Energy.
Nothing More.

MORNING THOUGHTS

Today: Mood:

Today's Prayer For Myself:

Today I Am Repeating To Myself:

What I Am Doing For Myself Today:

NIGHTLY THOUGHTS

Today's Inner Self Care Regime Included:

I Am Happy I Did:

Today I Gave Myself The Following Compliment:

Today I Was Inspired By:

I Increased My Confidence By:

Today I Protected My Space By:

MORNING THOUGHTS

Today: Mood:

Today's Prayer For Myself:

Today I Am Repeating To Myself:

What I Am Doing For Myself Today:

NIGHTLY THOUGHTS

Today's Inner Self Care Regime Included:

I Am Happy I Did:

Today I Gave Myself The Following Compliment:

Today I Was Inspired By:

I Increased My Confidence By:

Today I Protected My Space By:

MORNING THOUGHTS

Today: Mood:

Today's Prayer For Myself:

Today I Am Repeating To Myself:

What I Am Doing For Myself Today:

NIGHTLY THOUGHTS

Today's Inner Self Care Regime Included:

I Am Happy I Did:

Today I Gave Myself The Following Compliment:

Today I Was Inspired By:

I Increased My Confidence By:

Today I Protected My Space By:

MORNING THOUGHTS

Today: Mood:

Today's Prayer For Myself:

Today I Am Repeating To Myself:

What I Am Doing For Myself Today:

NIGHTLY THOUGHTS

Today's Inner Self Care Regime Included:

I Am Happy I Did:

Today I Gave Myself The Following Compliment:

Today I Was Inspired By:

I Increased My Confidence By:

Today I Protected My Space By:

MORNING THOUGHTS

Today: Mood:

Today's Prayer For Myself:

Today I Am Repeating To Myself:

What I Am Doing For Myself Today:

NIGHTLY THOUGHTS

Today's Inner Self Care Regime Included:

I Am Happy I Did:

Today I Gave Myself The Following Compliment:

Today I Was Inspired By:

I Increased My Confidence By:

Today I Protected My Space By:

MORNING THOUGHTS

Today: Mood:

Today's Prayer For Myself:

Today I Am Repeating To Myself:

What I Am Doing For Myself Today:

NIGHTLY THOUGHTS

Today's Inner Self Care Regime Included:

I Am Happy I Did:

Today I Gave Myself The Following Compliment:

Today I Was Inspired By:

I Increased My Confidence By:

Today I Protected My Space By:

MORNING THOUGHTS

Today: Mood:

Today's Prayer For Myself:

Today I Am Repeating To Myself:

What I Am Doing For Myself Today:

NIGHTLY THOUGHTS

Today's Inner Self Care Regime Included:

I Am Happy I Did:

Today I Gave Myself The Following Compliment:

Today I Was Inspired By:

I Increased My Confidence By:

Today I Protected My Space By:

MORNING THOUGHTS

Today: Mood:

Today's Prayer For Myself:

Today I Am Repeating To Myself:

What I Am Doing For Myself Today:

NIGHTLY THOUGHTS

Today's Inner Self Care Regime Included:

I Am Happy I Did:

Today I Gave Myself The Following Compliment:

Today I Was Inspired By:

I Increased My Confidence By:

Today I Protected My Space By:

MORNING THOUGHTS

Today: Mood:

Today's Prayer For Myself:

Today I Am Repeating To Myself:

What I Am Doing For Myself Today:

NIGHTLY THOUGHTS

Today's Inner Self Care Regime Included:

I Am Happy I Did:

Today I Gave Myself The Following Compliment:

Today I Was Inspired By:

I Increased My Confidence By:

Today I Protected My Space By:

WHAT I ACCEPT ABOUT MYSELF

They Said I Am

GREAT.

I Always Knew I Was Great.

I Now See The
WORLD
From A Different Perspective. Look How Far I've Come.

MORNING THOUGHTS

Today: Mood:

Today's Prayer For Myself:

Today I Am Repeating To Myself:

What I Am Doing For Myself Today:

NIGHTLY THOUGHTS

Today's Inner Self Care Regime Included:

I Am Happy I Did:

Today I Gave Myself The Following Compliment:

Today I Was Inspired By:

I Increased My Confidence By:

Today I Protected My Space By:

MORNING THOUGHTS

Today: Mood:

Today's Prayer For Myself:

Today I Am Repeating To Myself:

What I Am Doing For Myself Today:

NIGHTLY THOUGHTS

Today's Inner Self Care Regime Included:

I Am Happy I Did:

Today I Gave Myself The Following Compliment:

Today I Was Inspired By:

I Increased My Confidence By:

Today I Protected My Space By:

MORNING THOUGHTS

Today: Mood:

Today's Prayer For Myself:

Today I Am Repeating To Myself:

What I Am Doing For Myself Today:

NIGHTLY THOUGHTS

Today's Inner Self Care Regime Included:

I Am Happy I Did:

Today I Gave Myself The Following Compliment:

Today I Was Inspired By:

I Increased My Confidence By:

Today I Protected My Space By:

MORNING THOUGHTS

Today: Mood:

Today's Prayer For Myself:

Today I Am Repeating To Myself:

What I Am Doing For Myself Today:

NIGHTLY THOUGHTS

Today's Inner Self Care Regime Included:

I Am Happy I Did:

Today I Gave Myself The Following Compliment:

Today I Was Inspired By:

I Increased My Confidence By:

Today I Protected My Space By:

WHAT IS MAKING ME HAPPY RIGHT NOW?

MORNING THOUGHTS

Today: Mood:

Today's Prayer For Myself:

Today I Am Repeating To Myself:

What I Am Doing For Myself Today:

NIGHTLY THOUGHTS

Today's Inner Self Care Regime Included:

I Am Happy I Did:

Today I Gave Myself The Following Compliment:

Today I Was Inspired By:

I Increased My Confidence By:

Today I Protected My Space By:

MORNING THOUGHTS

Today: Mood:

Today's Prayer For Myself:

Today I Am Repeating To Myself:

What I Am Doing For Myself Today:

NIGHTLY THOUGHTS

Today's Inner Self Care Regime Included:

I Am Happy I Did:

Today I Gave Myself The Following Compliment:

Today I Was Inspired By:

I Increased My Confidence By:

Today I Protected My Space By:

MORNING THOUGHTS

Today: Mood:

Today's Prayer For Myself:

Today I Am Repeating To Myself:

What I Am Doing For Myself Today:

NIGHTLY THOUGHTS

Today's Inner Self Care Regime Included:

I Am Happy I Did:

Today I Gave Myself The Following Compliment:

Today I Was Inspired By:

I Increased My Confidence By:

Today I Protected My Space By:

MORNING THOUGHTS

Today: Mood:

Today's Prayer For Myself:

Today I Am Repeating To Myself:

What I Am Doing For Myself Today:

NIGHTLY THOUGHTS

Today's Inner Self Care Regime Included:

I Am Happy I Did:

Today I Gave Myself The Following Compliment:

Today I Was Inspired By:

I Increased My Confidence By:

Today I Protected My Space By:

I No Longer Stop
Anything Great
From Happening To Me. I

WELCOME

It All In.

MORNING THOUGHTS

Today: Mood:

Today's Prayer For Myself:

Today I Am Repeating To Myself:

What I Am Doing For Myself Today:

NIGHTLY THOUGHTS

Today's Inner Self Care Regime Included:

I Am Happy I Did:

Today I Gave Myself The Following Compliment:

Today I Was Inspired By:

I Increased My Confidence By:

Today I Protected My Space By:

MORNING THOUGHTS

Today: Mood:

Today's Prayer For Myself:

Today I Am Repeating To Myself:

What I Am Doing For Myself Today:

NIGHTLY THOUGHTS

Today's Inner Self Care Regime Included:

I Am Happy I Did:

Today I Gave Myself The Following Compliment:

Today I Was Inspired By:

I Increased My Confidence By:

Today I Protected My Space By:

MORNING THOUGHTS

Today: Mood:

Today's Prayer For Myself:

Today I Am Repeating To Myself:

What I Am Doing For Myself Today:

NIGHTLY THOUGHTS

Today's Inner Self Care Regime Included:

I Am Happy I Did:

Today I Gave Myself The Following Compliment:

Today I Was Inspired By:

I Increased My Confidence By:

Today I Protected My Space By:

A MUSIC PLAYLIST THAT DESCRIBES WHO I CURRENTLY AM AND HOW I FEEL

1.

2.

3.

4.

5.

6.

7.

8.

9.

10.

11.

12.

MORNING THOUGHTS

Today: Mood:

Today's Prayer For Myself:

Today I Am Repeating To Myself:

What I Am Doing For Myself Today:

NIGHTLY THOUGHTS

Today's Inner Self Care Regime Included:

I Am Happy I Did:

Today I Gave Myself The Following Compliment:

Today I Was Inspired By:

I Increased My Confidence By:

Today I Protected My Space By:

MORNING THOUGHTS

Today: Mood:

Today's Prayer For Myself:

Today I Am Repeating To Myself:

What I Am Doing For Myself Today:

NIGHTLY THOUGHTS

Today's Inner Self Care Regime Included:

I Am Happy I Did:

Today I Gave Myself The Following Compliment:

Today I Was Inspired By:

I Increased My Confidence By:

Today I Protected My Space By:

MORNING THOUGHTS

Today: Mood:

Today's Prayer For Myself:

Today I Am Repeating To Myself:

What I Am Doing For Myself Today:

NIGHTLY THOUGHTS

Today's Inner Self Care Regime Included:

I Am Happy I Did:

Today I Gave Myself The Following Compliment:

Today I Was Inspired By:

I Increased My Confidence By:

Today I Protected My Space By:

MORNING THOUGHTS

Today: Mood:

Today's Prayer For Myself:

Today I Am Repeating To Myself:

What I Am Doing For Myself Today:

NIGHTLY THOUGHTS

Today's Inner Self Care Regime Included:

I Am Happy I Did:

Today I Gave Myself The Following Compliment:

Today I Was Inspired By:

I Increased My Confidence By:

Today I Protected My Space By:

UNCONDITIONAL LOVE TOWARDS ME LOOKS AND FEELS LIKE

MORNING THOUGHTS

Today: Mood:

Today's Prayer For Myself:

Today I Am Repeating To Myself:

What I Am Doing For Myself Today:

NIGHTLY THOUGHTS

Today's Inner Self Care Regime Included:

I Am Happy I Did:

Today I Gave Myself The Following Compliment:

Today I Was Inspired By:

I Increased My Confidence By:

Today I Protected My Space By:

MORNING THOUGHTS

Today: Mood:

Today's Prayer For Myself:

Today I Am Repeating To Myself:

What I Am Doing For Myself Today:

NIGHTLY THOUGHTS

Today's Inner Self Care Regime Included:

I Am Happy I Did:

Today I Gave Myself The Following Compliment:

Today I Was Inspired By:

I Increased My Confidence By:

Today I Protected My Space By:

MORNING THOUGHTS

Today: Mood:

Today's Prayer For Myself:

Today I Am Repeating To Myself:

What I Am Doing For Myself Today:

NIGHTLY THOUGHTS

Today's Inner Self Care Regime Included:

I Am Happy I Did:

Today I Gave Myself The Following Compliment:

Today I Was Inspired By:

I Increased My Confidence By:

Today I Protected My Space By:

MORNING THOUGHTS

Today: Mood:

Today's Prayer For Myself:

Today I Am Repeating To Myself:

What I Am Doing For Myself Today:

NIGHTLY THOUGHTS

Today's Inner Self Care Regime Included:

I Am Happy I Did:

Today I Gave Myself The Following Compliment:

Today I Was Inspired By:

I Increased My Confidence By:

Today I Protected My Space By:

MORNING THOUGHTS

Today: Mood:

Today's Prayer For Myself:

Today I Am Repeating To Myself:

What I Am Doing For Myself Today:

NIGHTLY THOUGHTS

Today's Inner Self Care Regime Included:

I Am Happy I Did:

Today I Gave Myself The Following Compliment:

Today I Was Inspired By:

I Increased My Confidence By:

Today I Protected My Space By:

Shout Out To

ME.

The Real MVP.

My Soul, My Mind & My Spirit

NOW
UNDERSTAND

Each Other.

MORNING THOUGHTS

Today: Mood:

Today's Prayer For Myself:

Today I Am Repeating To Myself:

What I Am Doing For Myself Today:

NIGHTLY THOUGHTS

Today's Inner Self Care Regime Included:

I Am Happy I Did:

Today I Gave Myself The Following Compliment:

Today I Was Inspired By:

I Increased My Confidence By:

Today I Protected My Space By:

MORNING THOUGHTS

Today: Mood:

Today's Prayer For Myself:

Today I Am Repeating To Myself:

What I Am Doing For Myself Today:

NIGHTLY THOUGHTS

Today's Inner Self Care Regime Included:

I Am Happy I Did:

Today I Gave Myself The Following Compliment:

Today I Was Inspired By:

I Increased My Confidence By:

Today I Protected My Space By:

MORNING THOUGHTS

Today: Mood:

Today's Prayer For Myself:

Today I Am Repeating To Myself:

What I Am Doing For Myself Today:

NIGHTLY THOUGHTS

Today's Inner Self Care Regime Included:

I Am Happy I Did:

Today I Gave Myself The Following Compliment:

Today I Was Inspired By:

I Increased My Confidence By:

Today I Protected My Space By:

MORNING THOUGHTS

Today: Mood:

Today's Prayer For Myself:

Today I Am Repeating To Myself:

What I Am Doing For Myself Today:

NIGHTLY THOUGHTS

Today's Inner Self Care Regime Included:

I Am Happy I Did:

Today I Gave Myself The Following Compliment:

Today I Was Inspired By:

I Increased My Confidence By:

Today I Protected My Space By:

MORNING THOUGHTS

Today: Mood:

Today's Prayer For Myself:

Today I Am Repeating To Myself:

What I Am Doing For Myself Today:

NIGHTLY THOUGHTS

Today's Inner Self Care Regime Included:

I Am Happy I Did:

Today I Gave Myself The Following Compliment:

Today I Was Inspired By:

I Increased My Confidence By:

Today I Protected My Space By:

The Only Thing I
Chase Are My
GOALS.

I Don't Take Anything
PERSONAL,
Because I Personally Know Me.

MORNING THOUGHTS

Today: Mood:

Today's Prayer For Myself:

Today I Am Repeating To Myself:

What I Am Doing For Myself Today:

NIGHTLY THOUGHTS

Today's Inner Self Care Regime Included:

I Am Happy I Did:

Today I Gave Myself The Following Compliment:

Today I Was Inspired By:

I Increased My Confidence By:

Today I Protected My Space By:

MORNING THOUGHTS

Today: Mood:

Today's Prayer For Myself:

Today I Am Repeating To Myself:

What I Am Doing For Myself Today:

NIGHTLY THOUGHTS

Today's Inner Self Care Regime Included:

I Am Happy I Did:

Today I Gave Myself The Following Compliment:

Today I Was Inspired By:

I Increased My Confidence By:

Today I Protected My Space By:

MORNING THOUGHTS

Today: Mood:

Today's Prayer For Myself:

Today I Am Repeating To Myself:

What I Am Doing For Myself Today:

NIGHTLY THOUGHTS

Today's Inner Self Care Regime Included:

I Am Happy I Did:

Today I Gave Myself The Following Compliment:

Today I Was Inspired By:

I Increased My Confidence By:

Today I Protected My Space By:

THE THINGS I SAY TO MYSELF ARE......

MORNING THOUGHTS

Today: Mood:

Today's Prayer For Myself:

Today I Am Repeating To Myself:

What I Am Doing For Myself Today:

NIGHTLY THOUGHTS

Today's Inner Self Care Regime Included:

I Am Happy I Did:

Today I Gave Myself The Following Compliment:

Today I Was Inspired By:

I Increased My Confidence By:

Today I Protected My Space By:

MORNING THOUGHTS

Today: Mood:

Today's Prayer For Myself:

Today I Am Repeating To Myself:

What I Am Doing For Myself Today:

NIGHTLY THOUGHTS

Today's Inner Self Care Regime Included:

I Am Happy I Did:

Today I Gave Myself The Following Compliment:

Today I Was Inspired By:

I Increased My Confidence By:

Today I Protected My Space By:

MORNING THOUGHTS

Today: Mood:

Today's Prayer For Myself:

Today I Am Repeating To Myself:

What I Am Doing For Myself Today:

NIGHTLY THOUGHTS

Today's Inner Self Care Regime Included:

I Am Happy I Did:

Today I Gave Myself The Following Compliment:

Today I Was Inspired By:

I Increased My Confidence By:

Today I Protected My Space By:

MORNING THOUGHTS

Today: Mood:

Today's Prayer For Myself:

Today I Am Repeating To Myself:

What I Am Doing For Myself Today:

NIGHTLY THOUGHTS

Today's Inner Self Care Regime Included:

I Am Happy I Did:

Today I Gave Myself The Following Compliment:

Today I Was Inspired By:

I Increased My Confidence By:

Today I Protected My Space By:

Nothing Anyone Can Say Can

CHANGE

What I Think About Me.

MORNING THOUGHTS

Today: Mood:

Today's Prayer For Myself:

Today I Am Repeating To Myself:

What I Am Doing For Myself Today:

NIGHTLY THOUGHTS

Today's Inner Self Care Regime Included:

I Am Happy I Did:

Today I Gave Myself The Following Compliment:

Today I Was Inspired By:

I Increased My Confidence By:

Today I Protected My Space By:

MORNING THOUGHTS

Today: Mood:

Today's Prayer For Myself:

Today I Am Repeating To Myself:

What I Am Doing For Myself Today:

NIGHTLY THOUGHTS

Today's Inner Self Care Regime Included:

I Am Happy I Did:

Today I Gave Myself The Following Compliment:

Today I Was Inspired By:

I Increased My Confidence By:

Today I Protected My Space By:

MORNING THOUGHTS

Today: Mood:

Today's Prayer For Myself:

Today I Am Repeating To Myself:

What I Am Doing For Myself Today:

NIGHTLY THOUGHTS

Today's Inner Self Care Regime Included:

I Am Happy I Did:

Today I Gave Myself The Following Compliment:

Today I Was Inspired By:

I Increased My Confidence By:

Today I Protected My Space By:

MORNING THOUGHTS

Today: Mood:

Today's Prayer For Myself:

Today I Am Repeating To Myself:

What I Am Doing For Myself Today:

NIGHTLY THOUGHTS

Today's Inner Self Care Regime Included:

I Am Happy I Did:

Today I Gave Myself The Following Compliment:

Today I Was Inspired By:

I Increased My Confidence By:

Today I Protected My Space By:

MORNING THOUGHTS

Today: Mood:

Today's Prayer For Myself:

Today I Am Repeating To Myself:

What I Am Doing For Myself Today:

NIGHTLY THOUGHTS

Today's Inner Self Care Regime Included:

I Am Happy I Did:

Today I Gave Myself The Following Compliment:

Today I Was Inspired By:

I Increased My Confidence By:

Today I Protected My Space By:

Change is
GOOD.
I Feel Like Me.

I FEEL MOST ENERGIZED WHEN...

MORNING THOUGHTS

Today: Mood:

Today's Prayer For Myself:

Today I Am Repeating To Myself:

What I Am Doing For Myself Today:

NIGHTLY THOUGHTS

Today's Inner Self Care Regime Included:

I Am Happy I Did:

Today I Gave Myself The Following Compliment:

Today I Was Inspired By:

I Increased My Confidence By:

Today I Protected My Space By:

MORNING THOUGHTS

Today: Mood:

Today's Prayer For Myself:

Today I Am Repeating To Myself:

What I Am Doing For Myself Today:

NIGHTLY THOUGHTS

Today's Inner Self Care Regime Included:

I Am Happy I Did:

Today I Gave Myself The Following Compliment:

Today I Was Inspired By:

I Increased My Confidence By:

Today I Protected My Space By:

MORNING THOUGHTS

Today: Mood:

Today's Prayer For Myself:

Today I Am Repeating To Myself:

What I Am Doing For Myself Today:

NIGHTLY THOUGHTS

Today's Inner Self Care Regime Included:

I Am Happy I Did:

Today I Gave Myself The Following Compliment:

Today I Was Inspired By:

I Increased My Confidence By:

Today I Protected My Space By:

I LOVE TO SPEND
MY DAYS

MORNING THOUGHTS

Today: Mood:

Today's Prayer For Myself:

Today I Am Repeating To Myself:

What I Am Doing For Myself Today:

NIGHTLY THOUGHTS

Today's Inner Self Care Regime Included:

I Am Happy I Did:

Today I Gave Myself The Following Compliment:

Today I Was Inspired By:

I Increased My Confidence By:

Today I Protected My Space By:

MORNING THOUGHTS

Today: Mood:

Today's Prayer For Myself:

Today I Am Repeating To Myself:

What I Am Doing For Myself Today:

NIGHTLY THOUGHTS

Today's Inner Self Care Regime Included:

I Am Happy I Did:

Today I Gave Myself The Following Compliment:

Today I Was Inspired By:

I Increased My Confidence By:

Today I Protected My Space By:

MORNING THOUGHTS

Today: Mood:

Today's Prayer For Myself:

Today I Am Repeating To Myself:

What I Am Doing For Myself Today:

NIGHTLY THOUGHTS

Today's Inner Self Care Regime Included:

I Am Happy I Did:

Today I Gave Myself The Following Compliment:

Today I Was Inspired By:

I Increased My Confidence By:

Today I Protected My Space By:

MORNING THOUGHTS

Today: Mood:

Today's Prayer For Myself:

Today I Am Repeating To Myself:

What I Am Doing For Myself Today:

NIGHTLY THOUGHTS

Today's Inner Self Care Regime Included:

I Am Happy I Did:

Today I Gave Myself The Following Compliment:

Today I Was Inspired By:

I Increased My Confidence By:

Today I Protected My Space By:

I AM
EYE CATCHING.
I Am Mind Blowing.

MORNING THOUGHTS

Today: Mood:

Today's Prayer For Myself:

Today I Am Repeating To Myself:

What I Am Doing For Myself Today:

NIGHTLY THOUGHTS

Today's Inner Self Care Regime Included:

I Am Happy I Did:

Today I Gave Myself The Following Compliment:

Today I Was Inspired By:

I Increased My Confidence By:

Today I Protected My Space By:

MORNING THOUGHTS

Today: Mood:

Today's Prayer For Myself:

Today I Am Repeating To Myself:

What I Am Doing For Myself Today:

NIGHTLY THOUGHTS

Today's Inner Self Care Regime Included:

I Am Happy I Did:

Today I Gave Myself The Following Compliment:

Today I Was Inspired By:

I Increased My Confidence By:

Today I Protected My Space By:

MORNING THOUGHTS

Today: Mood:

Today's Prayer For Myself:

Today I Am Repeating To Myself:

What I Am Doing For Myself Today:

NIGHTLY THOUGHTS

Today's Inner Self Care Regime Included:

I Am Happy I Did:

Today I Gave Myself The Following Compliment:

Today I Was Inspired By:

I Increased My Confidence By:

Today I Protected My Space By:

MORNING THOUGHTS

Today: Mood:

Today's Prayer For Myself:

Today I Am Repeating To Myself:

What I Am Doing For Myself Today:

NIGHTLY THOUGHTS

Today's Inner Self Care Regime Included:

I Am Happy I Did:

Today I Gave Myself The Following Compliment:

Today I Was Inspired By:

I Increased My Confidence By:

Today I Protected My Space By:

MORNING THOUGHTS

Today: Mood:

Today's Prayer For Myself:

Today I Am Repeating To Myself:

What I Am Doing For Myself Today:

NIGHTLY THOUGHTS

Today's Inner Self Care Regime Included:

I Am Happy I Did:

Today I Gave Myself The Following Compliment:

Today I Was Inspired By:

I Increased My Confidence By:

Today I Protected My Space By:

I Am Not
REPLACEABLE.
I Am Not Forgettable.

THE WORDS I NEED TO HEAR RIGHT NOW ARE

MORNING THOUGHTS

Today: Mood:

Today's Prayer For Myself:

Today I Am Repeating To Myself:

What I Am Doing For Myself Today:

NIGHTLY THOUGHTS

Today's Inner Self Care Regime Included:

I Am Happy I Did:

Today I Gave Myself The Following Compliment:

Today I Was Inspired By:

I Increased My Confidence By:

Today I Protected My Space By:

MORNING THOUGHTS

Today: Mood:

Today's Prayer For Myself:

Today I Am Repeating To Myself:

What I Am Doing For Myself Today:

NIGHTLY THOUGHTS

Today's Inner Self Care Regime Included:

I Am Happy I Did:

Today I Gave Myself The Following Compliment:

Today I Was Inspired By:

I Increased My Confidence By:

Today I Protected My Space By:

MORNING THOUGHTS

Today: Mood:

Today's Prayer For Myself:

Today I Am Repeating To Myself:

What I Am Doing For Myself Today:

NIGHTLY THOUGHTS

Today's Inner Self Care Regime Included:

I Am Happy I Did:

Today I Gave Myself The Following Compliment:

Today I Was Inspired By:

I Increased My Confidence By:

Today I Protected My Space By:

MORNING THOUGHTS

Today: Mood:

Today's Prayer For Myself:

Today I Am Repeating To Myself:

What I Am Doing For Myself Today:

NIGHTLY THOUGHTS

Today's Inner Self Care Regime Included:

I Am Happy I Did:

Today I Gave Myself The Following Compliment:

Today I Was Inspired By:

I Increased My Confidence By:

Today I Protected My Space By:

SOME OF MY BEST CHARACTER TRAITS ARE

MORNING THOUGHTS

Today: Mood:

Today's Prayer For Myself:

Today I Am Repeating To Myself:

What I Am Doing For Myself Today:

NIGHTLY THOUGHTS

Today's Inner Self Care Regime Included:

I Am Happy I Did:

Today I Gave Myself The Following Compliment:

Today I Was Inspired By:

I Increased My Confidence By:

Today I Protected My Space By:

MORNING THOUGHTS

Today: Mood:

Today's Prayer For Myself:

Today I Am Repeating To Myself:

What I Am Doing For Myself Today:

NIGHTLY THOUGHTS

Today's Inner Self Care Regime Included:

I Am Happy I Did:

Today I Gave Myself The Following Compliment:

Today I Was Inspired By:

I Increased My Confidence By:

Today I Protected My Space By:

MORNING THOUGHTS

Today: Mood:

Today's Prayer For Myself:

Today I Am Repeating To Myself:

What I Am Doing For Myself Today:

NIGHTLY THOUGHTS

Today's Inner Self Care Regime Included:

I Am Happy I Did:

Today I Gave Myself The Following Compliment:

Today I Was Inspired By:

I Increased My Confidence By:

Today I Protected My Space By:

MORNING THOUGHTS

Today: Mood:

Today's Prayer For Myself:

Today I Am Repeating To Myself:

What I Am Doing For Myself Today:

NIGHTLY THOUGHTS

Today's Inner Self Care Regime Included:

I Am Happy I Did:

Today I Gave Myself The Following Compliment:

Today I Was Inspired By:

I Increased My Confidence By:

Today I Protected My Space By:

MORNING THOUGHTS

Today: Mood:

Today's Prayer For Myself:

Today I Am Repeating To Myself:

What I Am Doing For Myself Today:

NIGHTLY THOUGHTS

Today's Inner Self Care Regime Included:

I Am Happy I Did:

Today I Gave Myself The Following Compliment:

Today I Was Inspired By:

I Increased My Confidence By:

Today I Protected My Space By:

MORNING THOUGHTS

Today: Mood:

Today's Prayer For Myself:

Today I Am Repeating To Myself:

What I Am Doing For Myself Today:

NIGHTLY THOUGHTS

Today's Inner Self Care Regime Included:

I Am Happy I Did:

Today I Gave Myself The Following Compliment:

Today I Was Inspired By:

I Increased My Confidence By:

Today I Protected My Space By:

I LOOK FORWARD TO GIVING MYSELF

MORNING THOUGHTS

Today: Mood:

Today's Prayer For Myself:

Today I Am Repeating To Myself:

What I Am Doing For Myself Today:

NIGHTLY THOUGHTS

Today's Inner Self Care Regime Included:

I Am Happy I Did:

Today I Gave Myself The Following Compliment:

Today I Was Inspired By:

I Increased My Confidence By:

Today I Protected My Space By:

MORNING THOUGHTS

Today: Mood:

Today's Prayer For Myself:

Today I Am Repeating To Myself:

What I Am Doing For Myself Today:

NIGHTLY THOUGHTS

Today's Inner Self Care Regime Included:

I Am Happy I Did:

Today I Gave Myself The Following Compliment:

Today I Was Inspired By:

I Increased My Confidence By:

Today I Protected My Space By:

MORNING THOUGHTS

Today: Mood:

Today's Prayer For Myself:

Today I Am Repeating To Myself:

What I Am Doing For Myself Today:

NIGHTLY THOUGHTS

Today's Inner Self Care Regime Included:

I Am Happy I Did:

Today I Gave Myself The Following Compliment:

Today I Was Inspired By:

I Increased My Confidence By:

Today I Protected My Space By:

I Am At
PEACE.

I Know Longer Allow Anyone To
Shake My Peace.

MORNING THOUGHTS

Today: Mood:

Today's Prayer For Myself:

Today I Am Repeating To Myself:

What I Am Doing For Myself Today:

NIGHTLY THOUGHTS

Today's Inner Self Care Regime Included:

I Am Happy I Did:

Today I Gave Myself The Following Compliment:

Today I Was Inspired By:

I Increased My Confidence By:

Today I Protected My Space By:

MY THOUGHTS

MORNING THOUGHTS

Today: Mood:

Today's Prayer For Myself:

Today I Am Repeating To Myself:

What I Am Doing For Myself Today:

NIGHTLY THOUGHTS

Today's Inner Self Care Regime Included:

I Am Happy I Did:

Today I Gave Myself The Following Compliment:

Today I Was Inspired By:

I Increased My Confidence By:

Today I Protected My Space By:

MORNING THOUGHTS

Today: Mood:

Today's Prayer For Myself:

Today I Am Repeating To Myself:

What I Am Doing For Myself Today:

NIGHTLY THOUGHTS

Today's Inner Self Care Regime Included:

I Am Happy I Did:

Today I Gave Myself The Following Compliment:

Today I Was Inspired By:

I Increased My Confidence By:

Today I Protected My Space By:

MORNING THOUGHTS

Today: Mood:

Today's Prayer For Myself:

Today I Am Repeating To Myself:

What I Am Doing For Myself Today:

NIGHTLY THOUGHTS

Today's Inner Self Care Regime Included:

I Am Happy I Did:

Today I Gave Myself The Following Compliment:

Today I Was Inspired By:

I Increased My Confidence By:

Today I Protected My Space By:

MORNING THOUGHTS

Today: Mood:

Today's Prayer For Myself:

Today I Am Repeating To Myself:

What I Am Doing For Myself Today:

NIGHTLY THOUGHTS

Today's Inner Self Care Regime Included:

I Am Happy I Did:

Today I Gave Myself The Following Compliment:

Today I Was Inspired By:

I Increased My Confidence By:

Today I Protected My Space By:

MORNING THOUGHTS

Today: Mood:

Today's Prayer For Myself:

Today I Am Repeating To Myself:

What I Am Doing For Myself Today:

NIGHTLY THOUGHTS

Today's Inner Self Care Regime Included:

I Am Happy I Did:

Today I Gave Myself The Following Compliment:

Today I Was Inspired By:

I Increased My Confidence By:

Today I Protected My Space By:

MORNING THOUGHTS

Today: Mood:

Today's Prayer For Myself:

Today I Am Repeating To Myself:

What I Am Doing For Myself Today:

NIGHTLY THOUGHTS

Today's Inner Self Care Regime Included:

I Am Happy I Did:

Today I Gave Myself The Following Compliment:

Today I Was Inspired By:

I Increased My Confidence By:

Today I Protected My Space By:

MORNING THOUGHTS

Today: Mood:

Today's Prayer For Myself:

Today I Am Repeating To Myself:

What I Am Doing For Myself Today:

NIGHTLY THOUGHTS

Today's Inner Self Care Regime Included:

I Am Happy I Did:

Today I Gave Myself The Following Compliment:

Today I Was Inspired By:

I Increased My Confidence By:

Today I Protected My Space By:

I Push Myself
To Become
BETTER.

I Am Becoming Better.

I Like That I

DON'T

NEED

Everyone To Like Me.

THE THINGS I'VE GOT TO DO FOR ME

MORNING THOUGHTS

Today: Mood:

Today's Prayer For Myself:

Today I Am Repeating To Myself:

What I Am Doing For Myself Today:

NIGHTLY THOUGHTS

Today's Inner Self Care Regime Included:

I Am Happy I Did:

Today I Gave Myself The Following Compliment:

Today I Was Inspired By:

I Increased My Confidence By:

Today I Protected My Space By:

MORNING THOUGHTS

Today: Mood:

Today's Prayer For Myself:

Today I Am Repeating To Myself:

What I Am Doing For Myself Today:

NIGHTLY THOUGHTS

Today's Inner Self Care Regime Included:

I Am Happy I Did:

Today I Gave Myself The Following Compliment:

Today I Was Inspired By:

I Increased My Confidence By:

Today I Protected My Space By:

MORNING THOUGHTS

Today: Mood:

Today's Prayer For Myself:

Today I Am Repeating To Myself:

What I Am Doing For Myself Today:

NIGHTLY THOUGHTS

Today's Inner Self Care Regime Included:

I Am Happy I Did:

Today I Gave Myself The Following Compliment:

Today I Was Inspired By:

I Increased My Confidence By:

Today I Protected My Space By:

I Act Like It
Doesn't Affect

ME.

But Deep Down Inside,
It Doesn't Affect Me.

MORNING THOUGHTS

Today: Mood:

Today's Prayer For Myself:

Today I Am Repeating To Myself:

What I Am Doing For Myself Today:

NIGHTLY THOUGHTS

Today's Inner Self Care Regime Included:

I Am Happy I Did:

Today I Gave Myself The Following Compliment:

Today I Was Inspired By:

I Increased My Confidence By:

Today I Protected My Space By:

MORNING THOUGHTS

Today: Mood:

Today's Prayer For Myself:

Today I Am Repeating To Myself:

What I Am Doing For Myself Today:

NIGHTLY THOUGHTS

Today's Inner Self Care Regime Included:

I Am Happy I Did:

Today I Gave Myself The Following Compliment:

Today I Was Inspired By:

I Increased My Confidence By:

Today I Protected My Space By:

MORNING THOUGHTS

Today: Mood:

Today's Prayer For Myself:

Today I Am Repeating To Myself:

What I Am Doing For Myself Today:

NIGHTLY THOUGHTS

Today's Inner Self Care Regime Included:

I Am Happy I Did:

Today I Gave Myself The Following Compliment:

Today I Was Inspired By:

I Increased My Confidence By:

Today I Protected My Space By:

Made in the USA
Columbia, SC
30 December 2019